Blue Ribbon.Team

Laurie Dougherty, CAE, CTF

Copyright © 2017 Laurie Dougherty
All rights reserved.
ISBN: 1548437883
ISBN-13: 978-1548437886

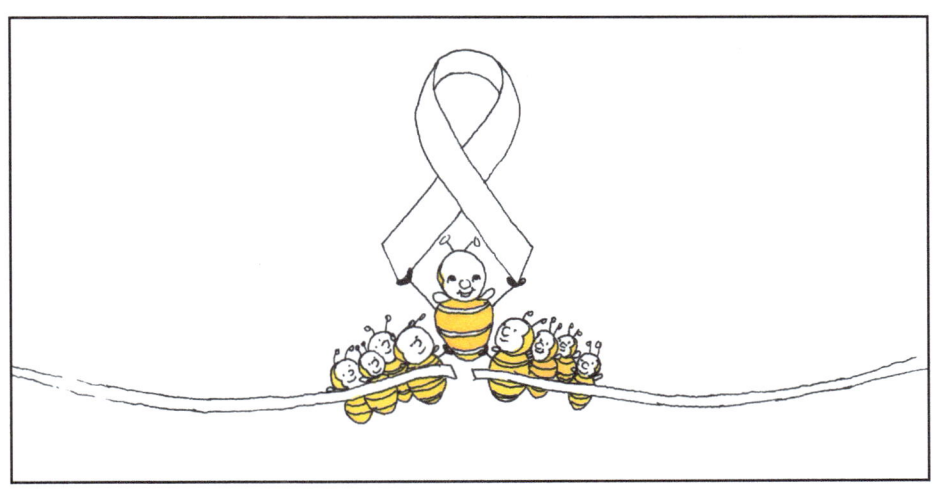

DEDICATION

Over the time of my career, I have spend one year's worth of days in or planning meetings. We can't live without meetings, but we can sure make the most of them by following a few simple guidelines.

This book is designed to assist teams in completing a self assessment and developing a self improvement plan to maximize meeting effectiveness. Follow the simple steps outlined in this book and people will be standing in line to volunteer to work on your team.

Use this book effectively

This book contains a self assessment for your team as well as the templates for an improvement plan. Take small incremental steps to improve your team's effectiveness.

In addition to the copies in this book, you will find downloadable copies of the templates for self evaluation and self-improvement at www.BlueRibbon.Team

CONTENTS

Chapter 1 Why BLUE RIBBON? 1

Chapter 2 Have A Clear Direction 3

Chapter 3 Before Your Meeting 5

Chapter 4 During the Meeting 8

Chapter 5 Follow Up 12

Chapter 6 Foster Growth 14

Chapter 7 Technology 17

Summary 20

Team Assessment 21

Improvement Example 23

Improvement Template 24

ACKNOWLEDGMENTS

Thank you to the Illinois Section American Water Works Association Committee Members, Board Members and other Executive Directors that provided feedback on this publication.

Thank you to the countless people who have attended meetings from which we have learned that using these techniques makes a difference.

Last but not least, thanks to Rich who relentlessly heard me say, "I have to get the book finished." Thank you for your never ending support and encouragement.

Thank you to our wonderful illustrator, Susanne Nason living in Atlantic Canada. She illustrates books, teaches, lectures and mentors. She is committed to sharing her knowledge with others as they explore their own creative potential. To find out more, visit her website; susannenasonillustration.com or look for her on Facebook at Susanne Nason Illustration.

WHY BLUE RIBBON?

The **Blue Ribbon** is a symbol of high quality. The association comes from The Blue Riband, a prize awarded for the fastest crossing of the Atlantic Ocean by passenger liners. Prior to that it was from Cordon Bleu, which referred to the blue ribbon worn by a particular order of knights.

The spelling blue riband is still encountered in most English-speaking countries, but in the United States, the term was altered to Blue Ribbon, and ribbons of this color came to be awarded for first place in certain athletic or other competitive endeavors. It also may be applied to distinguished members of a group or commission who have convened to address a situation or problem; the usual usage is "blue ribbon commission" or "Blue-Ribbon panel". "wikipedia"

> "If you want to go quickly, go alone.
> If you want to go far, go together."
>
> ~African proverb.

People work in teams for a reason. Whether they are volunteering on a cause that they feel strongly about or, assigned to a team, they all want to feel that their time has been well spent. They all want to make a difference.

Following the guidelines to achieve the status of a Blue Ribbon Team will maximize the impact of your group as well as encourage participation and fun along the way.

Not every team will be able to achieve every goal outlined in this book. The more best practices your team can implement, the more effective the performance of your team. We recommend that your team members complete the evaluation located in the appendix to start a baseline score for your team. You can then measure your progress incrementally until your team becomes a Blue Ribbon Team.

Blue Ribbon Team provides sample best practices for committee practices for both in person and virtual meetings. Many teams these days are primarily virtual and we have provided tips to especially enhance online meetings.

> "It always seems impossible until it is done."
>
> *Nelson Mandela*

HAVE A CLEAR DIRECTION

Know Why Your Team Exists
Be sure that your team knows and agrees why you exist. What will be different in your organization or association as a result of the work of your team? The more "effect" your work has on the outcomes, the greater the commitment of your team. Agree upon the goals of your team and when new initiatives are brought before the team by a member, measure them against the goals which you agreed upon.

☑ **Review the Overarching Goals** - Review the goals at the highest level of your organization or association. Determine that your team supports the overall goals of the organization.

☑ **What Do You Want to Change?** - Determine first what change you want to effect. Start with the end in mind. If you want to have more "engagement" in your community, state that. A goal of having more engagement in the community will gather more commitment than an individual social event. The social event is the "activity" that supports the goal.

☑ **Determine Activities** - Determine what activities will be the most catalytic for your goal. If there was one "action" that got you closer to your goal, and it has a person to champion it, give priority to that activity. Having early successes will create excitement for the rest of the activities to come.

Typical Pitfalls

🚫 **Not being realistic** – If you have 3 people on your team, you cannot achieve the same as a team with 20 active members. Be realistic when you list for your activities to support your goals. Establish a quick time line for a "reality check".

🚫 **Trying to do too much** – If you have a goal that seems to be intangible, break it down into smaller tangible goals. Instead of 2 large goals, consider 8 smaller achievable goals.

🚫 **Getting off track** - Committee members sometimes get so excited about a new opportunity that the group follows their excitement and delays working on the goals you have already established. Don't let the excitement of the moment sway you from your path. Put the new item on the burner for a later date.

BEFORE YOUR MEETING

No Agenda – No Meeting
A good measure of a meeting is the amount of time that the leader speaks vs. the time that the participates speak. Today's typical meeting consists of an agenda sent out hours before the meeting, followed by a leader who tells everyone what they were supposed to have finished by this time and frustrated that no one is talking or contributing.
The leader may feel as though their committee is not supporting them. When what is really happening, is the leader is not creating the atmosphere and process to allow the members to participate.

Agendas
Agendas serve as a road maps and notification to the participants such as: what to expect at the upcoming meeting, reminder of the meeting time, date, and particulars such as phone number or screen sharing URL. It also sets the priorities of what work should be done; however,

the first items on the agenda are not always the most important. Many times the first items are "checklist" items or "wins" for the committees. It is encouraging for the team to have some agenda items that are easy to achieve and quick to review.

☑ **Every meeting has an icebreaker:** An ice breaker provides an opportunity for each participant to have their voice heard. Include the ice breaker first on the agenda. It doesn't matter whether your meeting is in person or online. You can make ice breakers fun. Having a laugh at the beginning of the meeting is a good start. If you are in a virtual meeting, it provides a "sound check." An ice breaker is also a great way to start the meeting on time and yet allow for those who are 5 minutes late to not have missed crucial information.

☑ **Provide estimated times:** Each agenda item should have an estimated time allowed. It will help you to know if you are off track and can then decide to delay extended discussions on an item to a future meeting.

☑ **Be specific:** List specific items. Do not use generic terms such as: Ice breaker, meeting reports, closing and next meeting. It appears that you are avoiding putting thought into the process of creating the agenda. List specifics as much as possible.

☑ **Next steps:** Each agenda should include an area for next steps. Include in the next steps, what, who, when and what is the expected outcome and how will it be used.

☑ **Next meeting:** At the end of each meeting allow time to set the next meeting date and time. Many times, people tend to "set up a doodle poll" for the next meeting. If you have a majority of your team on the call, respect their participation and ask them to check their calendars at that time for scheduling the next meeting.

A sample timed agenda is listed below.

Time	Item	Person	Outcome
8:00 am	Ice Breaker	Chair	Check in - voice check
8:10 am	Item #1 Specifics	Person #1	Decision, etc.
8:25 am	Next Steps	Chair	Action items
8:30 am	Next Meeting	Chair	Date, time, details

Typical Pitfalls - Agendas

🚫 **Too many items on the agenda.** Plan in advance how long items should take and be realistic.

🚫 **Be true to your participants.** If your agenda is too full and you don't get to "everything" you have disrespected your participants time and participation.

🚫 **Not specific enough.** Each meeting's agenda should not look the same. Be specific in your items. Give enough detail to encourage someone to attend rather than thinking it is the same as last meeting.

🚫 **No action items.** If there are no action items on your agenda, don't have the meeting. Send a report instead. If you do not need input from your team, you are simply updating them on a project. You do not need a meeting.

🚫 **Not indicating who is reporting out.** Team members that have worked on a project should be entitled to share their progress first with team members. Each agenda item should be attributed to different people. Spread the work as much as possible.

Success Magazine states, "70% of executives feel that meetings are a waste of time." Don't let your meetings become a statistic.

DURING THE MEETING

You Have Two Ears and One Mouth
When your team members show up for a meeting whether online or in person, they expect to "make a difference." A good measure of good meeting participation is to ask yourself, "Did I hear everyone's voice at least once?" At the end of the meeting, each person needs to feel that they had an impact, a voice and their time and energy made a difference.

Let's Not All Speak at Once
We want to hear from all meeting participants, just not at the same time. Here are a few methods for both in person and online meetings to invite structured participation. You want to gain agreement in the beginning of your meeting on how you will proceed.

☑**In Person Meetings** - The most important issue is that you have a way to identify those who want to speak and a process to stop them from going on and on. Following are some suggested techniques.

- **Talking Stick** - whoever is holding the stick is talking. When they are done talking they hold the stick out for someone to take and also have their chance for input. You can also use a ball that you can toss across the room. The person holding the ball has the floor.

- **Sideways Name Tents** - Ask participants to turn their name tents on end to signal that they would like to talk.

- **Raised Hand** - the old fashioned way of raising your hand to speak.

- **Around the Room** - Ask each person to give a "twitter version" 140 characters of their input. Demonstrate how you would like them to answer.

☑ **For Online Meetings** - Use the best available technology, and learn its characteristics before the meeting. You don't want to be learning it as you use it. Practice with another person.

- **Verbally Signal You Are Complete** - Ask the participants to state their name when speaking and when they are finished speaking, state "I am complete, or I'm done, or that's all." It provides a signal that their thought process is complete and they are done.

- **Use The Attendee Roster** - Ask for individual verbal input by going up and down the roster of names. If you vary the order and starting point, you will keep people's attention as the don't know when you may start with them.

- **Chat Boxes** - Use chat boxes for the participants to type in their answers. Ask everyone to type at the same time. This allows for individual idea generation. Ask for volunteers to read the input or the authors to read their input when called upon.

- **Use Polls** - For items that need to have a choice, use the online polling. From picking a date for your next meeting or deciding which items to work on next, polling is a democratic and quick way to make a decision.

☑ **Gathering Input from All** - Ask your team members to take a role in the meeting. If your meeting is a manageable size, call on each of the team members by name to give input. If you have too many people to take the time gather input from each member, you can use the following techniques.

- **In Person Meetings** - Have participants brainstorm individually on paper a list of responses to your question. Then have each person select their top 3 choices and share their choices with a partner or small group. Ask the small groups to forward their top 4-6 items that they agree upon. Write the groups' output onto a flip chart or projected document. This allows each team member to have a voice in the process and their ideas heard in the small group discussions while moving the discussion forward.

- **For Online Meetings** - Use chat boxes for the participants to type in their answers. Ask everyone to type at the same time. Ask a volunteer to read the list of entries an ask the participants if there are any areas that need clarification. Optionally, have each person read what they typed. They are likely to automatically give a slightly longer description of their ideas.

- **Use Online Break Out Rooms.** This technique if available in your online service takes some practice but yields great results. The breakout rooms are able to collaborate with the same techniques as above. You can them bring them all back to the main meeting and share the individual breakout data.

⊘ Typical Pitfalls – Meeting Management

- **Being late** – As the leader of the team, you should be at the meeting early. For an online meeting, tune in 5-7 minutes ahead of time. For an in person meeting arrive 30 minutes prior. This will give you an opportunity to avoid any last minute technical issues, connect with those who are also early and give you a few minutes to focus on your agenda. Many times, new members are concerned about being late and they will be early to avoid embarrassment. This gives you an opportunity to talk to them.

- **Talking too much** – Don't talk all of the time. Consider yourself a conductor in an orchestra. You are directing the team efforts. Let them play the music.

FOLLOW UP

Follow up until you get ANY response

People need to be reminded. With all good intentions, they simply get busy. It is likely they intended to do what they said. If you follow up in time for them to fulfill their commitment, they will be able to participate in the meeting. Also, they will know you are looking forward to their input and that their ideas are valued.

☑ Blue Ribbon Practices – Follow Up

- Set a reminder for yourself to review your agenda and action items and reminders 15 days prior to your meeting.

- Cue up an outbound email reminder with the date to be sent. Many email systems will allow you to "stage" an email.

- Send a personal note to those who volunteered to do something. Tell them you are looking forward to their project report, offer to help, be supportive.

- Use an interactive easy-to-use tracking system such as ASANA that will allow your committee members to respond to tasks, ask questions and enter into a dialogue in between meetings.

- Set an example and complete the tasks that you have assigned yourself on a timely basis. If you cannot, delegate them to a team member who can.

- Give team members an opportunity to quit. No one wants to be the one that says "I quit." But some people take on more than they are able to handle. When given the opportunity to "step away" graciously, many will take advantage of that opportunity. It will also leave them with a good feeling and they will look forward to when their schedule allows them to return to your team.

- Ask attending team members to reach out to specific people to bring them up to date on what happened in the meeting. Create a "buddy" system. The missing person may be more likely to tell their "buddy" they just don't have time to participate and want to leave the group.

- Have an annual check-in process for commitment for the year. Ask team members to specifically respond to what they would like to be involved with for the coming year. Indicate that if there is no response, we will understand that they do not want to be involved in the team activities at this time. Set and agree to participation expectations of team members.

FOSTER GROWTH

Strive to make your job obsolete - Your goal as the team leader is to develop your team to function at a level in which they rely on you less and less. You want them to all be accountable for what they commit to and to follow through. The way to get commitment is to expect it and reinforce it. If you ask a team member to do something and then don't follow up, they will know they can just ignore your request and you will forget.

☑**Blue Ribbon Practices - Foster Team Growth**:

- **Alternate Acting Chairs** - Have others "chair the meeting" on a rotating basis. Select an interval in which others run the meeting. Coordinate the agenda and let the substitute leader take control and support them.

- **Alternate Meeting Venues** – If you always meet online at the same time each month, you may be missing out on someone who could participate. Considering every other meeting the day and time of your meetings to allow a wider participation. For those the primarily meet online, schedule an in-person meeting quarterly if possible.

- **Accept that not everyone does it like you do.** Team members all perform at different levels. In a volunteer role, their best may be not as good as your best. Consider that their best is good enough. Consider that it may be more important to have them experience success as a part of your committee rather than criticism. Does the job they did achieve the end result? If so, let it go.

- **Use Subcommittees** - Have team leaders for "projects" within your team. Let that person take the lead on those projects. Do not try to inject your opinions on how it should be done. Encourage those teams to meet outside of regular meetings and report on their progress at the team meetings.

- **Recruit a Vice Chair** - This will allow you to occasionally miss a meeting. In fact, consider intentionally missing a few meetings and allow your vice chair to assume the role. Collaborate in between meetings with your vice chair on the direction of your team and ask for specific input. Value their opinions and work as a team. Having a vice chair will allow you extra coverage and you are less likely to have to cancel a meeting. Also a vice chair will most likely be the next chair of the committee and your team will lose less time reorganizing themselves.

- **Celebrate Success** - Have fun with your team. Celebrate your successes both large and small. Give yourself a round of applause or a pat on the back. Use shirts or pins to create a team feeling. Many times people join a committee because they noticed the committee members wearing shirts. They wanted to be one of those "wearing the shirts." A small denomination gift card or hand written "thank you" or "congratulations" note will go a long way to encourage participation.

- **Don't Do Everything** – Don't try and do everything at one time. Take on projects only as you have willing team members to champion them. If you talk about a project at a meeting and everyone says it is a "great idea" and yet no one volunteers to champion it, maybe it was not such a "great idea". Or possibly it needed to be broken down into bite size pieces.

- **Create a Diverse and Inclusive Committee** - Assess the personal and professional backgrounds of your committee members. Recruit additional committee members, as needed to create a well-rounded representation of the general membership of your committee. Create an inclusive environment by encouraging all committee members to share their ideas. Provide respect and consideration to new and varied perspectives in the course of the committee activities.

- **Recruit for Specific Skills and Knowledge** – Conduct an "inventory" of your committee members. See what knowledge or relationship building gaps you have. Seek out specific members to join your team that have those skills or relationships. Consider it similar to recruiting for a professional sport and having members who are strong in different areas.

> "If you think you are too small to make a difference, try sleeping with a mosquito."
>
> *Dalai Lama*

TECHNOLOGY

Technology is your friend.
Technology needs to be easy to use, accessible across many platforms, affordable, secure and flexible. The minute you think you have selected the best technology for your online meetings, there will be new platforms to take its place. Your team members appreciate learning new technologies from you. It is an opportunity for them to safely experiment with new technologies as a participant in your meetings.

☑ **Blue Ribbon Practices - Technology**

- **Be a participant and a leader** - If you can, use a separate computer to show you the "participants" view. Login as a participant and compare the screen view from a participant's point of view vs a presenter/facilitator point of view.

- **Audio Controls** - Many of the free conference call systems offer a visual dashboard. It will tell you who is on the call and where background noise is coming from. Announce at the beginning of the meeting that you have the ability to mute individual lines should the background noise be too great. These dashboards are free and included with the free accounts.

- **Turn Off the Hello Beep** - If you are using a dashboard, you can see if someone new has joined. Even if you are not using the dashboard, it is not critical that you know each person who is late. It's very frustrating for a team member to be on time for a meeting and have you, as the leader, restart the meeting each time a latecomer joins. You are disrespecting those who were on time. You can announce that for those who are late to the meeting, you will stay on after the call for any reviews.

- **Invite Participants Early for "Coffee"** - Whether you are online or in person, make a note that you are inviting them to arrive 10 minutes early to visit. The social part of the meeting is more important for some than others. Allow them to meet early and share stories or have virtual coffee.

- **Close Out UN-Necessary Programs** - Close down (not minimize) any programs you will not be using during the meeting. If you feel you need to watch for in bound emails, use your phone email and not your computer email. You want to minimize the programs running while conducting an online meeting. Also, if you are screen sharing, you don't want the notification that you are high bidder on your eBay auction to appear during the meeting.

- **If Everyone Is Muted** - Send a video recording. Seriously - if all of your participants are muted, why are you having a meeting? You can record your own video presentation and ask them to watch at their leisure. If you have a fear that they will not watch it, offer a contest for those who answer the most right questions regarding the meeting.

- **Record the Meeting** - If you are not talking about anything private, consider recording the meeting. If you use Adobe Connect, each "layout" is a separate chapter and those who watch the recording can skip directly to the chapter that affects them. If you record just the audio, you will offer a pod-cast like opportunity for those driving in their car to listen to the playback of the audio. If you are recording, announce to the participants that you are starting and ending the recording. If you are recording audio only, be sure and read out loud any text typed on the screen so that those who listen later do not rely on the screen for clarity.

- **Offer a Phone Only Option** - Although we prefer that all participants are screen sharing, some are just too busy and want to connect via their Blue tooth speaker in the car while driving. If you do not accommodate that request, that person will begin to feel that they cannot participate and will drop off. With any technology that you use, offer the option to use their phone. Do not require them to use computer speakers. Many offices do not offer a computer speaker headset for privacy.

SUMMARY

PEOPLE SUPPORT WHAT THEY CREATE

When you work as part of a team, you are able to achieve what would be impossible alone. Not only will your team achieve greatness, they will enjoy the journey. Team members will make new lifelong friends, learn new technical and leadership skills and grow both individually and professionally. People who want to be part of something bigger than themselves will continue to search out opportunities until they find a "home" where they feel appreciated, respected and included. Create a "Blue Ribbon Team" and you will earn their commitment.

A Blue Ribbon Team Assessment sheet can be found in the appendix of this book. Copy it and share it with your team members. Average your team scores to see how you are currently performing.

Test your team to determine your beginning score and re-test/review again every six months. Use the template in the index to Develop your "Team Management Improvement" plan to increase involvement and participation.

Electronic copies of the Blue Ribbon Team Assessment sheet and Team Improvement Plan can be found at www.BlueRibbon.Team
Provide your team with Blue Ribbon Team ribbons. Teams that score an average of 120 or more are eligible for free ribbons for your team. Submit your score summary and request your ribbons at www.BlueRibbon.Team

> "People support what they create."
>
> *Margaret J. Wheatley*

TEAM ASSESSMENT

Team Self Evaluation

Have each of your team members complete this evaluation and average the overall scores. On each statement, rank your team's performance on a scale of 1 to 10. 1 is not doing it at all and 10 is the standard practice for your team. Re-evaluate your team from time to time see how you have improved.

Question	Score
Our team has written goals that have been shared with the team members	
Our team's goals support the overall organization goals	
Our team's projects have "champions" other than the team leader or chair.	
Our meetings include an opening ice breaker for creating inclusive environment.	
Our agenda items have amount of time for each item.	
At the end of each meeting, we have identified next steps and who is responsible.	
Our team has a process to keep everyone from talking at the same time.	
Our team leader reminds the members of their commitments at least a week prior to the meeting.	
Our team uses an online tracking software such as ASANA for projects.	
Our team leader follows up regularly on missing committee members.	
Our team uses sub-committees for projects and leaders are accountable	
Our team has a vice-chair that can step in at any meeting.	
Our team has fun and recognizes successes large and small.	
Our meetings start on time and don't restart whenever someone is late.	
Total number of points………..	

HOW DID YOUR TEAM SCORE?

1-25	Sorry - You need a new team leader.
26-50	Your team leader needs to evaluate how they are managing the team.
51-75	Your team is trying to keep the group together – suggest that you pick one or two items and work on those for improvement.
76-100	Your team is doing well but there is room for growth.
101-120	Your team is on the verge of achieving greatness – just tweak a few practices.
121-140	Your team is performing well. Continue to mentor team members for succession.

If you scored 120 or greater, submit your team's average score sheet with your name, mailing address and number of Blue Ribbons you would like. The ribbons will be sent to you free of charge.

Your team can proudly wear their ribbons to your next event to share and celebrate that they are a Blue Ribbon Team.

If your team did not score 120 or better, I encourage you to develop a team improvement plan on the following page.

TEAM IMPROVEMENT PLAN EXAMPLE

Directions: Circle the areas in the self evaluation that scored 7 or lower. Using the chart below, develop an action plan for improving each of those areas. You may want to make copies of the improvement plan template and use one sheet for per area of improvement. Digital oopies can be found at www.BlueRibbon.Team

Your Score	Area of Improvement
7	Our teams' projects have "champions" other than the leaders.
Date Completed	**Improvement Steps**
	Review current projects and prioritize
	Gain commitment from the team
	Seek out a project champion
	Determine reporting system for project team
	Re-evaluate in 6 months

TEAM IMPROVEMENT PLAN DIRECTIONS
One Sheet per area of improvement

Circle the areas in the self evaluation that scored 7 or lower. Using the chart below, develop an action plan for improving each of those areas. Digital oopies can be found at www.BlueRibbon.Team

Your Score	Area of Improvement
Date Completed	Improvement Steps
	Re-evaluate and assess improvement

Laurie Dougherty, CAE, CTF

ToP Qualified Trainer, Certified Technology of Participation Facilitator (CTF), understands non-profits and government agencies. She currently serves as Executive Director of a non profit 501c3 and has over 24 years of experience working with non profit organizations, volunteers and boards of directors.

Laurie earned her Certified Association Executive (CAE) designation in 2013 and is a Technology of Participation (ToP) ® Methods Trainer and Facilitator. She was the first U.S. qualified trainer for the Institute of Cultural Affairs, Canada's "Meetings That Work."

While most people dread meetings, Laurie's passion for a well-run meeting is only matched by her "out-of-the-box" thinking. She is able to re-tool and re-energize committees and organizations. Laurie's current knowledge of methods, trends and technology are an asset to her facilitating skills in getting participants to think out of their comfort zone.

Laurie has coordinated many events from strategic planning sessions for non-profits, to large and small grant funded community events. She has assisted with national conference planning. And is a trained professional facilitator for both in-person and virtual meetings using a variety of tools.

Education and Certifications
Certified Association Executive (CAE)
ToP Facilitation Methods, Strategic Planning, Environmental Scanning, Virtual Facilitation, Facilitation Graphics
ToP Qualified Trainer
ToP Certified Facilitator (CTF)
FoCuSed Facilitation
Certificate in Non Profit Management - UIC

Affiliations
Florida Society of Association Executives
American Society of Association Executives
Illinois Society of Executive Directors
Meeting Professionals International
American Water Works Association
Mid-Atlantic Association of Facilitators
International Association of Facilitators
ToP Network

Contact: Laurie Dougherty, 2388 SE 17th Terr., Homestead, FL 33035
Email: LaurieDougherty@me.com

NOTES

NOTES

www.ingramcontent.com/pod-product-compliance
Lightning Source LLC
Chambersburg PA
CBHW041210180526
45172CB00006B/1224